THE SAILOR
OF THE
SEVEN SEAS

Translated from the original Bangla Sat Sagorer Majhi By Yasmin Faruque

FARRUKH AHMAD

Order this book online at www.trafford.com
or email orders@trafford.com

Most Trafford titles are also available at major online book retailers.

Printed in the United States of America.

ISBN: 978-1-4669-9648-9 (sc)
ISBN: 978-1-4669-9649-6 (e)

Trafford rev. 06/12/2013

 www.trafford.com

North America & international
toll-free: 1 888 232 4444 (USA & Canada)
phone: 250 383 6864 ♦ fax: 812 355 4082

Dedication

To my father, Dr. R. A. Ghani

And mother, the late Mrs Hosne Ara Ghani

Whose love has been, is and always will be inspiring for me.

Contents

Acknowledgements

This book would be sadly incomplete if I do not acknowledge the assistance and encouragement I received from quite a few people. Thanks are due to Professor Motiur Rahman, President, Farrukh Academy, Dhaka, for graciously permitting me to translate this beautiful book. I am thankful to my parents for their love and encouragement. To my husband, Dr. Saleh Faruque, thanks are due for bequeathing the lion's share of his free time to the best presentation my little book could hope for. To my darling son, Shams, I say thanks for being my most ardent supporter.

Biography of the Poet

Farrukh Ahmad was born in the village of Majh Ail, in Sreepur of Magura district, Bangladesh, on June 10, 1918. His father was Khan Sahib Syed Hatem Ali, and mother, Roushan Akhtar. In 1924, when Farrukh was only five years old, his mother died.

His schooling began in his small village open-air school. Then he attended the Kolkata Model M.E. School and the Baliganj High School. He graduated, however, from the Khulna Zilla School, passing in the First Division, in 1937. At high school, he had as teachers such noted writers as the poet Ghulam Mustafa, writer Abul Fazal, and the poet Abul Hashim. At Baliganj he had among his classmates Prasun Kumar Dey, poet of note, and Satyajit Roy, later a popular writer and filmmaker.

In 1937, his first poem 'Ratri' appeared in the magazine 'Bulbul,' edited by Habibullah Bahar (August). Another poem 'Pap Janma' came out in the periodical 'Muhammadi' edited by Mohammad Akram Khan, the same month. His first short story, 'Antarleen,' came out in the 'Muhammadi', too. He wrote the stories 'Biborno,' 'Mrito Basudha,' 'Ze Putul Dollyr Ma,' 'Procchonno Nayika,' etc., which came out one by one during 1937-9. When his teacher Abul Fazal went to Kolkata, Farrukh requested a copy of Walt Whitman's classic <u>Leaves of Grass</u>. Literary liaisons among Farrukh and the poet Ahsan Habib, writer Abu Rushd etc. were formed. Farrukh enrolled at Ripon College, Kolkata, where he had celebrities such as Vishnu

De, Buddhadev Basu, and Pramathanath Bishi etc. as teachers. At this time a bouquet of Farrukh's poetry was published in the magazine 'Kobita,' edited by Buddhadev Guha.

In 1938, an illustrated treatise entitled 'Mr. Jonab Ali to the Exercise Instructor' was published. Allama Sir Muhammad Iqbal, the philosopher-poet, passed away. Farrukh wrote a bouquet of poems entitled 'Smarani,' dedicated to the memory of Iqbal. Poem 'Andharer Swopno' came out in the monthly Saogat, published from Kolkata. Farrukh contributed regularly to this magazine until 1947.

In 1939, Farrukh passed his I.A. (Now H.S.C.) examinations, and got admitted to the Scottish Church College, Kolkata, in the Honors College of Philosophy, for the Bachelor's degree. Poets such as Suvash Mukherji and Fateh Lohani were classmates. World War II began.

In 1941, Farrukh quit Scottish Church College and got admitted to Kolkata City College with Honors in Bangla Literature. Rabindranath Tagore, the Universal Poet, passed away in August. Poetic Bangla translations of some Koranic verses are published entitled 'Kabye Koran.' The poet transformed some of his ideals in the light of the Lahore resolution of 1940.

In 1942, the poet tied the knot with his cousin Tayyeba Khatun. He wrote a poem entitled 'Upahar' on the occasion of his marriage; the poem was published in the 'Saogat.' Kazi Nazrul Islam, the Poet of National Awakening (Now Poet Laureate of Bangladesh) falls ill of an incurable disease.

In 1943, Farrukh joined the office of the IG Prisons. He recited the poems 'Dal Bandha Bulbuli' and 'Biday' at the seventh session of Bongiyo Mussalman Sahitya Sangsad. The poet began writing poems for Sat Sagorer Majhi, Sirajam Munira and Kafela. He also wrote poems on the drought of 1942-3.

<u>Sat Sagorer Majhi</u>, the poet's first volume of poems, was published in 1944. A poem entitled 'Lash' came out in the periodical 'Akal,' edited by the young poet Sukanto Bhattacharyya. Farrukh quit his job at the office of the IG Prisons to join the Kolkata Civil Supplies Office. His father, Syed Hatem Ali, died on Nov. 10.

Kazi Abdul Wadud, the spokesman for the Liberation of Intellect Movement, was hopeful about Farrukh's poetry in a speech at the Writers' Conference of PEN in 1945. Poems 'Shikar', 'Hey Nishanbahi' and 'Sat Sagorer Majhi' were published in the poetry journal 'Malancha', edited by Abdul Kadir and Rezaul Karim. The editorial emphasized Farrukh's poetry. The poet joined the staff of the periodical 'Muhammadi.' An untoward incident led to his resignation about a year later.

The poetry chapbook <u>Azad Karo Pakistan</u> was published in 1946. The poet recited a poem entitled 'Nijer Rokto' on Kolkata Radio. It may be mentioned here that the poet would participate in the program 'Golpodadur Ashor' on Akashbani Radio. The poet worked briefly at a company in Jalpaiguri.

-In 1947 Farrukh was unemployed after quitting his job at the 'Muhammadi'. This year the essay 'Navin Kobi Farrukh Ahmad' by the poet Abdul Kadir was broadcast from Kolkata Radio. The poet left Kolkata for his in-laws' place Durgapur, in Jashore. Essay, 'Pakistan: Rashtrovasha O Sahityo' was published. Colonial rule ended. Independence of 1947 was achieved.

The poet and his family moved permanently to Dhaka in 1948. He joined Dhaka Radio as a casual artist. He began to write songs for radio. In addition to modern, patriotic, Gospel and songs praising the Prophet, the poet gave short talks, and wrote skits, musicals and lyrical dramas. During the 50s, Farrukh began to direct Kishore Majlish, an educational program geared towards teen-agers. The prose-play 'Raj Rajra' is published. The historic Language Movement begins.

In 1951 Farrukh shunned the program to celebrate the birth anniversary of Iqbal, in protest of not inviting young writers.

In 1952, the book Sirajam Munira was published. Farrukh was hired as a staff artist of the Dhaka Radio. Barkat, Salam, Jabbar, Rafiq, Shafiq, Shafiul and many others embrace martyrdom, inciting protests at Dhaka University and outside, starting at Dhaka Radio. Farrukh emerged vocal. He participated in the Islamic Cultural Conference, held in Dhaka.

In 1953, Farrukh Ahmad was sacked from Dhaka Radio, along with fifteen others. The ensuing 17-day strike by these artists played a significant part in re-instating them all, including Farrukh.

In 1957, Farrukh was a key participant in the centenary observance of the Independence Movement of 1857, composing poems and songs on the occasion.

In 1958, the verse-play Naufel O Hatem was broadcast on Dhaka Radio. The play was produced by Khan Ataur Rahman, who also played the starring role.

In 1960, Farrukh was awarded the Pride of Performance Award by the Pakistani President. He also received the Bangla Academy Award for Poetry, and was elected a Fellow of the Academy. In the Drama Week of Bangla Academy, the verse-play 'Naufel O Hatem' was performed.

In 1961 Farrukh's verse-play Naufel O Hatem came out in print. Farrukh went on an extensive Governmental tour of North and South Bangla. The poet was accorded a heartfelt reception at Dhaka Hall, presided over by Prof. M. Abdul Hai. Syed Ali Ahsan, Prof.

Munir Chowdhury, poet Ahsan Habib, Abul Hossain et. al. spoke on Farrukh's poetry. Poet Shamsur Rahman, Muhammad Muniruzzaman, Salma Chowdhury, Badrul Hasan, Shabnam Mushtari et. al. recited Farrukh's poems. A program of Farrukh's songs directed by singer Abdul Ahad was put on. Dr. Sirajul Islam Chowdhury read the reception letter to Farrukh here.

In 1963 Farrukh's poetry book Muhurter Kobita was published. His satirical poetry was published under a pen name in the 'Dholaikabyo' edited by Faruque Mahmud. The School of Bangla Language and Literature at the Dhaka University observed Bangla Language and Literature Week. On this occasion recitations of poetry starting with the Charyyapada and up to & including Farrukh Ahmad's poetry were organized. Prof. Rafiqul Islam recited Farrukh's poem 'Dahuk' here.

In 1965, 'Pakhir Basha,' a book of juvenile poetry, was published. Inspired by the Indo-Pakistani war, the poet composed such inspirational songs as 'Jangi Jawan Chalo Bir,' 'Shaheeder Khunoranga Kashmir,' 'Jehader Maidane Chalo Jai.'

Hatem Ta'yi came out in 1966. The poet was awarded the UNESCO Prize for his book Pakhir Basha and the Adamjee Award for Hatem Ta'yi. The poet went for the last time to Faridpur, to see his elder brother, Syed Siddique Ahmad. On his return he wrote the poems 'Boishakh,' 'Padma,' and 'Aricha Parghate,' among other well-known and celebrated poems. The poet spurned the Sitara I Imtiaz title conferred by the Pakistani president as a sign of patriotism.

In 1968, 'Harafer Chharda', a book of kids' poems, was published.

In 1969 came the juvenile poetry book Notun Lekha. 'Kobi Farrukh Ahmad,' a well-researched book by Sunitikumar Mukherji, was published. Noted artist Mustafa Aziz painted a portrait of the poet. Countrywide popular uprising of 1969 began.

In 1970 came the rhyme book <u>Chhardar Ashor</u>, Part I. The poet completed more than two decades with Dhaka Radio. This year the poet was featured on the editorial and cover of the fortnightly Elan (Now Radio Bangla), for the early November issue. National elections took place.

In 1971, the poet recited a poem on Dhaka Radio for the very last time. Bangladesh came into being after a bloody struggle.

1973 saw Farrukh facing a catastrophic dilemma at work after the liberation of Bangladesh. Essayist Ahmad Safa wrote an acerbic article, 'Farrukh Ahmader Ki Oporadh?' (What Crime Has Farrukh Ahmad Committed?) (Gonokontho, June 15). As a result, Farrukh was re-instated in the commercial activities of Radio Bangladesh, Dhaka.

The poet suffered physically and mentally for many everyday and social reasons. In June 1974 he wrote his very last poem: Famine 1974(A Pictograph). Apart from this he wrote poems in praise of God the Almighty and of the Prophet Muhammad (PBUH) and poems on Gaddafi, and translated a long Urdu poem on Maulana Shafiullah (Dadaji). Farrukh breathed his last on Oct. 19, at home in Eskaton Gardens, Dhaka.

In 1975, <u>Farrukh Ahmader Shreshtho Kobita</u> was published. Farrukh was honored with a posthumous Ekushey Padak for Literature in 1977, the posthumous Swadhinata Puroshkar in 1980, and the Islamic Foundation Award in 1984.

Biography of the Translator

Yasmin Faruque was born on Nov. 11, 1955, in Dhaka, Bangladesh. She attended Viqarun Nisa Noon Girls' High School, Holy Cross College and the School of English Literature at Dhaka University, Bangladesh. She has written stories and poems since she was a mere child. The present work, Sailor of the Seven Seas, is her fourth attempt at translation. Her first, Moni Monjusha, a Bangla translation of short English poems, appeared in print in November 1979. Her second, Tribute to Tagore, a translation of Tagore's short stories, was published by Trafford in July 2012. Her third book, Accolades, a translation of Farrukh Ahmad's book Sirajam Munira, was published by Trafford Publishers in April 2013. Now married and the mother of an adult son, she lives in Grand Forks, ND, USA. Since 2005, she has presented stories, poems and essays at the Annual Writers' Conference at the University of North Dakota, Grand Forks. Eight of her book reviews were published in the Grand Forks Herald during 2005 and 2006.

Preface

Sat Sagorer Majhi, which I have translated into English as <u>The Sailor</u> <u>of the Seven Seas,</u> **is** a book of adventure poems by Farrukh Ahmad. These poems bear a striking resemblance to Tennyson's, for example the poem 'Sindbad (Sindbad the Sailor)', which resembles the main idea in Tennyson's poem 'Ulysses.' Like Tennyson's Ulysses, Farrukh Ahmad's Sindbad also exhorts Muslims to shake off lethargy and venture forth in quest of adventure.

Farrukh Ahmad was also a contemporary of Nobel Laureates Thomas Stearns Eliot and William Butler Yeats. As Eliot deplored the seeming abyss of nothingness that the world had fallen into, so did Farrukh Ahmad wring his hands in despair over the decline of effort and vivacity in Muslims. As Yeats looked back often to the past, so did Farrukh Ahmad. In this respects he can also be compared to Michael Madhusudan Dutta, the epic poet of Bangla Literature.

Farrukh can also be compared to Rebel Poet Kazi Nazrul Islam, the Poet Laureate of Bangladesh. The poems of both poets inspire Muslims to shake off lethargy and work for the betterment of the masses. Farrukh, like Nazrul, urges Muslims to forge ahead in progress. This book is my homage to Farrukh Ahmad. I know of no better way to pay homage to the greatest poet of Muslim Renaissance since Kazi Nazrul Islam.

It is very difficult to translate good poetry; even then, because I liked these poems so much, I wanted to share them with the English-speaking readers. I have tried to capture the same mood in my translations as the poet had in writing the originals. If my translations touch my readers' hearts as the originals did mine, I shall be amply rewarded. I hope my readers look with a forgiving eye on any inadvertent errors I may have made.

Yasmin Faruque

Grand Forks, ND, USA, 2013

SINDBAD THE SAILOR

(Original: Sindbad)

The colorful velvet days are past, now is the time
For a new voyage. I hear again
The salt sea calling. The silver-white moon
Floats atop the crest of the flood tide;
A wave as high as a hill bears forth
The call of the salt sea.
Now is the voyage on fresher waters,
O Sindbad, sailor!
Oh, that solid carpet of agate has been calling me
To the shore of the sky, between life and death.
After so long a time away
Who knows through what tides the voyage will pull me this time!
This senseless heart roams the intensely fragrant camphor copses,
The stone-hard black wood has put on ivory armor
The spicy breeze from the peepul thicket seems to lull me to sleep
While the fearless sea-eagle flies down
To the immersion in the ocean waters.
The velvet days have passed in enthusiasm
For fine doings
Even so, the wave of a distant journey floated to port.
O Mahout, please lift the howdah from the elephant
And finish off the ornate decoration
For today we have to dress in the blue battle fatigues
Of all combat seamen.

The expansive waters swell and hiss angrily like a great sea-snake.
In the mouth of the flood tide floats the little white boat,
And we know not what tide will engulf us again
Or where indeed the flood of new sunlight will open up again,
Where again the ship might be wrecked
And we might have to float out on planks, who knows for how long.
We don't know or care about that, the blue ocean has called.
Opening out the unconfined, sparkling horizon
The young soldier tills the water with his oar.
The sun revolves overhead; the moon makes her mark, too.
The deck of the boat buckles in the fierce storm
While we the fearless crew keep rowing all the year round.

OUT TO SEA
(Original: Ba'r Dariyay)

The snow white ocean liner gallops
from ocean to ocean like a swift racehorse!
Raising sparks with her stamping on the sharp oars
The snow-white schooner speeds from ocean to ocean . . .
The wind fills the sails like a lion's mane puffed
up, the moon swings atop the mast
All night the dreams seek out their way by the fire of starlight
The bark sails on apace, lively and unstoppable
Churning up the salt sea-water all the livelong night.
The sun is effaced as the evening star shines out over the horizon
The morning air touches my burning blood
The pulsing of dawn seems to grow ever fainter
And the sails bow down as a calming wind stirs them.
The sea eagle crosses, the madly-foaming night beside her
And the vibrant free blue morn glows on the dark backdrop
The bow of the wind blows in karfa rhythm on the steadfast mast
While the reckless sea-eagle soars in the sea-blue tempest
Molded by the cyclone, her form is graceful in the whirling winds
Her well-formed feathers reflect the slipping coral rainbow
She floats aimlessly all day, far afar
Bringing the song of spring back to sere gardens.
Liberation has rung out on the long coconut fronds
As on the shores of Sarandip the birds begin to sing.
Perhaps the sea-eagle seeks her nest among the sand-dunes

As the snow-white sea-horse gallops from ocean to ocean.
Where to now, to what port, O Pilot,
Will the stern of the boat turn?
Where will the white steamboat drop anchor?
Slicing through so many whirls and eddies, as if negligently
We've left behind mornings and evenings—red, blue and saffron
Our steed, with foaming mouth,
May not stop even when the tides do!
How restlessly eager she is to traverse the stormy field!
The oars ring out a blue intoxication on her tether
While in our hearts is the insanity of the ocean!
Where on earth is that tipsy vessel galloping to, like a comet?
Far afar, the port has merged into the horizon
The brightness of the sun fills the sails, as
The curved bow of a new path moves away in the gurgling of the sea.
Maybe the white cutter loses her way
In intense drunkenness and top speed!
In the distant port the bright sun measures our speed
Filled with inebriation and top speed are the ship's sails
Here in the green harem of the horizon float the fairies' songs
The ancient forest wakes dancing with her face hidden by the veil.
Towards the mirage of a desert river canters the blind sailboat!
Perhaps it's a mistake, or perhaps not
At the beginning of the storm the venom
and the apprehension gather.
O sailor, turn the tiller with the unmerciful touch!
Where do this road and this speed end,
And where, O where is the rudderless catamaran galloping to?
The dark typhoon clouds gather, the deck sways and heaves
Blue in fear, the faint murmur of the whirlpool,
The summer tempest to end all dreams ceases.

The very chains seem to neigh; the sails catch the typhoon winds
O Boatman, grasp the helm mercilessly!
Listen, O hill of fog, serpentine waves,
To the hissing of that hooded snake!
There trembles a horrible death!
Furl the sails; we have to sail through this storm
Even if the giant black sea snake flickers its tongue frequently . . .
The black billow comes flying like the minaret of Al Burj
A hill of waves breaks on deck as fast as lightning
O sailor, what darkness envelops the daytime sky!
Hark! There break billow upon billow of black waves,
Along with which the blue sky flashes its sword.
The sail rips, maybe the mast will break too
The storm whips the deck to whine plaintively.
O dear, is our white sailboat going to drown in this sea?
In the name of God the Almighty
O boatman, steer the boat like a man
Through these waves!
Even if the strong muscle of your skilled arm breaks down
Then go ahead and change hands quickly
Even a moment of negligence now
Can drown you out in a powerful storm.
Rein in this foaming whirlpool, crossing past this bluster
Sailing sea to sea, the tugboat shall find her way home.
So many oceans have you crost
Fighting maybe to save the boat from countless typhoons
Your veins have burst, a hand was torn clean away
Yet you turned the helm with your other hand,
Fighting the storm all the while.
O Sailor of the Seas! In your prowess is the heat enough to melt rock

God the Almighty has given you the power
to traverse these rocky ways.
Sail ahead, tearing through countless ocean waves,
Encircling these tides, themselves like Al Burj,
May your wheel flash out and your eyes sparkle
Where this mare floats out aimlessly on the current!
Stand you there, breaking the black wings of this tide.
Passing the pale and dusky night
White ship with sails unfurled will pull this floating home ashore.
The boatman will drop anchor once more on the dock of Sarandip.
The acquaintance with you deepens during the sea-storm
Breaking through the dark canopy of a myriad waves
You have grasped us, pulling us strongly ashore.
In the moonlight I have observed the coastline of my Sarandip.
If this time this cruise boat stops short
We shall cross this ocean on planks
Even if a thousand lives are lost, we shall not concede defeat.
Grasp the helm with a steady hand
Ne'er shall we doubt this last wave any more.
See, Boatswain, we stand here having vanquished the sea-storm
Only the seven hundred oarsmen have floated away, and
Only one wooden front deck has flown off
Behold, injured yet steady stands the mast
Measuring the edges of the open sea in a quiet dream.
Behold the budding stars in the sky
Where on the waters still as mirrors the Fairy Queen
Views her own reflection.
We are now in the realm of Khizir, who has conquered this storm
O Boatman, we have returned victorious after this time's tempest!
Behold our standard, flying against the blue sky
As if the white mare gallops on, with her mane swelled up like a sail.

LAST NIGHT AT SEA

There had been a storm during the night. In the dim light of the early dawn, the sea is now calm. Some downcast oarsmen come to stand around Sindbad on the deck of the ship.

1ST **OARSMAN**: Did you hear any noise,
   As you stayed awake last night?
   The mast and the oars rocked.

2ND **OARSMAN**: Perhaps the sea-hen, bereft
Of her mate, sat on the mast with a stormy heart.

3RD **OARSMAN**: It was as if the enormous
   Jinn enthralled by the chains
   Of the Prophet Suleiman
Beat his breast as he wept all night, all night
I heard those cries as I lay on deck wrapped
   In the sail all the livelong night.
His whole body was scarred with despair,
Maybe that captive Jinn wept for his distant homeland
Last night I heard his weeping in the murmur of the sea.
Along with that my heart too lamented
And sped to where my life was, in the port of Baghdad.

4TH **OARSMAN:** Beside the Tigris, at the tent entrance
Where my beautiful young dream lives, there sped my heart.

The flute of the caravan brought poisoned pain,
And I heard that unspoken pain of my
heart in the voice of that storm.

5TH **OARSMAN:** I clutched my chest as I lay
With my ears to the deck in that storm
And heard the song of the cradle hung on the fig-tree branch far afar
The newborn baby burst out crying hard on my breast
I heard that baby's cries in last night's storm.
Mate with me for seven voyages, you know, this fist of stone
Fell beside the cradle at that, weeping in pain
In unconsciousness, I sought two gentle wings in the dark.
I won't listen to any more nays, turn the bow of the boat right now.

SINDBAD: Can you hear the attraction of the distant homeland,
O my boatmen?
Is the sea-search at last at an end?
Is the deep love of the land calling you?

6TH **OARSMAN**: Awake alone last night, I
heard the storm wailing at the mast,
I heard the weeping in the distant fringes of the desert all the while
A lone nutshell had floated in with the storm-surge
All the layers of my heart surged too
A sea-rooster came with soil in its beak
The blood in my fiery veins melted into tears—
The salt sea-waters heaved in the dim light, and
The waves moaned in gut-wrenching pain;
I have heard and felt the pull of my old soil—
And I sought out my horizon by the starlight.

7ᵀᴴ **OARSMAN**: The moon of the white night calls
From the Baghdadi date-fronds
Perhaps the Mahgir spreads a web of moonshine on the sea,
Where the earth has set a trap of love with gentle mists.
Today is our time to return home.

SINDBAD: Taking possession of a new
Island, I have laid a foundation there.
I've surveyed the boundaries of the Seven Seas;
I've crost the typhoon and braved the storm
Descending onto Ruha Island we've healed the
termite-bites on our wounded bodies.
We have had to cross so many fearfully lonely oceans
Returning to our masts we lit the travel-lamps . . . .

1ˢᵀ **OARSMAN**:
List where Baghdad calls to us from afar off!
We shall go, piercing all the tides and turning all the bends
We've bought ivory and allspice
With diamonds and other gems we have filled our holds
We have done with selling peepul, chilis, and cardamom pods.
O friends of the sea, pray turn the boat around.

SINDBAD: Timid, weak . . .

2ᴺᴰ **OARSMAN**: We fear not, nor are we weak.

3ᴿᴰ **OARSMAN**: We are Muslim seamen, we fear not death!
We have got the empire of the sea, along with Khizir.
In these earthly powers, the soil and sweet memory
Of Baghdad stir. Dear friend, please turn the boat around now!

SINDBAD: In last night's bad storm, the mold of the blue sea
Revealed rare gems blooming like flowers of priceless jewels.
The attraction of the voyage pulls me far afar.
The canopy of sky over the salt sea is stirring near my heart.
The never-ending feeling of beauty in this,
God's seemingly endless universe
Solidifies thickly in a desire to travel distant lands
Like essence of diamonds . . . .

4TH **OARSMAN**: Perhaps so many lives were destroyed
In the ocean currents
A weary body . . . .

SINDBAD: Even so, Baghdad shall witness a new voyage
Again tomorrow, after a weary day.
Ah, you've forgotten the palace in the water,
Built of sea blue agate
Where the Princess of the Zilqad night, the
moon, descends thirteen layers
Having forgotten all her dreams and yearnings
And the fruition of her distant dreams.
Seed-stones are scattered on the carpet!
Your friend, the sailor Sindbad, calls once more
To pierce the canopy of the sky; so let's go!
Face to face with Black Death, we young warriors must return
To pull the raging storm out of the ocean-tides.
Forget not this life of the sailor
Begin the new voyage again today
See the new light we've lit on the mast;
The monsoon winds fill the sails and ring out.

5TH OARSMAN: We shall rest in my leafy hut just two moments,

Not forgetting the irresistible pull of the earth.

Where indeed, how far, is the port?

Where is the song of my date arbor?

6th OARSMAN: Out at sea we've sniffed the fresh smell of life.

We have found boatloads of nutmeg and myrrh.

Scarred by typhoons, we need to rest a while

Only seamen can understand the sympathy of the soil.

7TH OARSMAN: The ancient dilapidated

mind breaks down in a sea-cyclone

At the head of the green, green grass blows the constant wind.

The newly built clay hut of the mind does not break down

While the prow of the boat seeks her shelter-port.

8th OARSMAN: We've finished our trading, even with

Myriads of scars and hits upon our bodies.

SINDBAD: So, my friends of the sea, turn the boat around now.

(The oarsmen scurry in a noisy crowd towards the helm of the boat)

THE OARSMEN(IN CHORUS): So, my friends

of the sea, let us turn the boat around now.

SHAHRIYAR

(Original: Shahriyar)

The weary Simoom nerves have stopped
still at Shaherzadi's casement.
The wounded heart that finds the world empty
seeks the oasis in the Sahara Desert.
On this dead sere soil the pomegranate seeds will again take root.
Will it hold back the reins of black desire?
There seems to be no end to the errors of a chaotic evening tonight
We know that the soil of mistakes will not bloom forth with flowers.
A myriad signals have called forth.
The animal that ran with a painful life towards death
Submerging thousands of weak female faces in a tide of blood
Sped on yet, even as he blindly followed the completely wrong path.
I remember the beautiful loving mind of that new dawn
When my whole existence has been effaced
by the stigma of ignominy.
Splashes of red blood float in my whole spirit,
My body is putrid with gangrenous sores
And the blackest sin of covetousness rises in my mind.
The stars wail in Shahriyar's blue welkin . . . .
No longer do winey moonbeams awaken at mine head
Justice burns like fire in my breast
Just as if these are the trials of the grave
under the seven splendid canopies
Wrapped in costly raiment, wakes this mind that has lost everything
Seeking everywhere its heart's dearest;

Even the slightest wound awakens in this
heart the lament of loneliness,
The chronicle and songs of your myriad nights.
The moon holds that colorful dream
As the search for the melody awakens.

Dim and weary, on my barren pillow I listen
To the empty failure that the strings of the sitar hold.
I only recall the numerous mishaps.
Some illusory memory covering the layers of my body
Has shrouded my free blue edge
And my whole life now is a dirge.
My thirsting soul is a distant trader
Wanting now to build a home on the lost homestead
In new zeal.
The moon sets on her silver throne.
The mountain is on his knees.
O Hasin Banu, fill the new welkin
With the notes of vivacity.
And even yet I know this life of mine revolves
Like a sentence passed
And meets up with a weak, greedy wing on the winding path again
Wanting to be destroyed in the storm
He knows where the sun is, yet he wants to shroud it in a cloud
Again and again wishing to drown in a whirlpool
And poisoning each and every bend on the road of life.

THE CELESTIAL CAPTAIN
(Original: Akash Nabik)

In the walnut grove

And in the almond and apricot orchards

Thou pass thine days

O Bird of the pristine white comeliness!

On thine snow-white feathers do flash

The lightning and the rainbow—

Resplendent in gold, silver, pink and other hues.

Thou hast cut the sky in a faint line

Traversing numerous layers of light,

In sunshine, dew and salt water.

O Bird! Thou knew not fear and never did get scared.

In thine wings thou brought the pomegranate from Iranian orchards

Thine melody made the stars in the distant heavens dream,

And all of a sudden the pomegranate blossom unfurled her petals

Her pleasure, flushed in sweet embarrassment, broke all bounds.

Traversing the far horizon thou wake her in thy melody

In the walnut grove

And in the almond and apricot orchards.

The ripe cantaloupe, with the sweet juice in her heart,

Bursts forth,

Defeating even crystallized sugar in sweetness,

In the golden voice of thine she-parrot! Her eyes, like narcissi,

Seek her friend, with the petals of the pomegranate blossom.

Her days and nights are full of a tide of flowers;

On thine wings thy golden girl has chosen her own husband.

Days & nights passed in dreamy sweetness.

In deep emotion the narcissus has opened her eyes

In the walnut grove

And in the almond and apricot orchards.

The branches of the henna are abloom with bunches of blossoms

The moon of the twelfth night awakens behind the leaves.

On some solitary rosebush an agitated bulbul

Unleashes her melody in the moonlight,

flooding the embankment at night.

A night as dense as honey, peaceful, dreamy and enticing

Bringing to thine eyne tears of deep emotion

The weary she-parrot slumbers

As does the fading narcissus; only the jasmine is still awake

In the walnut grove

And in the almond and apricot orchards.

Thine morning glows in the eastern heavens like a blood-red dish

While the henna and the saffron are absolutely pure.

The just-awakened birds warble, twitter and chirp in glad agitation

And the full cup of the pomegranate blossom bursts with its juices.

The adventure to the horizon starts anew,

As do ever newer morning songs.

In the still sky, towards the sea far afar,

O Celestial Captain, awaken the pull of the tide.

I knew not when thou hadst fallen to the dust,

But today I hear the wind sighing as it blows.

Needlessly the shelled nut falls to the stones

And juicy apricots tumble to earth.

O Bird, only thou art not here.

Having flown off to a mildewed port of tears
Thou art not here, Bird.
Here at the casement of an untimely demise
O Bird! Thine groans rise to the heavens.
Thou behold the shaft-sharp glances
Of some famished eye,
And in the grey-black backdrop of despair
Up floats the port of death.
Thine she-parrot flies by herself somewhere
And near the snake's hood she falls senseless.
Thou canst not fly! Have the stars dimmed, too?
Have the ebb-tide storms of the moon obscured it, as well?
Does the dragon sway its head on thy road and sea?
Does the deadly tuberculosis spread further among thy ribs?
Thine song of wayfaring ended long ago
And the sun has dimmed
The envoy of thine moonlit nights has forgotten her golden voice.
Thou dost not hear the quiet evening whistle tranquilly here.
All thou hast after a weary day is the venom of a black night.
Thy light feathers do not fly in the tempest
But keep on bending and breaking forever.
O, homeless in the hungry famine!
All the doors are closed to her; where has she a place indeed
At this unfamiliar port?
The bird does not return to her familiar nest
In the walnut grove
And in the almond and apricot orchards.

Has the beating storm made her forget
That very well-known nest of hers?

Has the storm defeated her, indeed?
The heart-wrenching, grief-stricken moan
of the she-parrot floats in the air.
Has defeat neared her life?
O Bird! Ne'er in life wert thou fearful
Or accepted defeat!
The clear liberty of the seven heavens! Did the fangs of black night
Consume thee as thou slept?
Even then I know that thou canst transcend this ignoble death.
Why then art thou still here?
O bird, smite this chain resoundingly hard
And bring liberal freedom to the fields of the Seven Heavens,
And tarry not one moment more here.
Thou wert not supposed to accept defeat, O Bird!
The free flag of thine song has flown all over the sky
The stars in the distant sky watch this defeat.
Everyone is so astonished at the way thou art losing!
O Bird, thou realize not that this is only fatigue
A momentary oblivion spreads in front of thee
as sand dunes and desert
Thou behold only the poison of a night parching with thirst
And not the oasis of sweet water towards the rising sun.
Has the moon set? Is she not visible in the dark?
O Bird! The white line of thy stars has not gone out, yet.
Thine moonlight has not dimmed yet either
In the walnut grove
And in the almond and apricot orchards.

Thou hast to return there today,
Bypassing this sick tubercular lethargy

And traversing this lightning sky that rends the sky asunder

This dark night has to be tilled

To fill this sterile desert with pomegranate buds.

We have to bring new seeds by voyaging to distant Faran

To saturate this hard soil with that high tide.

Then this burthen of thine fragrance has
been touched ever and anon.

I did not crave thee as I floated away on the tide of fire.

Today I seek thee ardently

In leaf, twig and grass, yet find thee not.

Only the scent wafts in from afar

Soaking the field and the mind in the momentary pink breath.

But then in that momentarily-lit field

I get thee not.

Today its scent comes; mine thirsting heart in the breath of the night

I know is also thine, so a very long time ago indeed

Majnoon went forth, carrying the licking flames of youth in his breast

At Lailee's behest

To the grey world beyond worlds.

They have drawn and left behind the layers,

And the Sahara laughed with the oasis at her heart.

Perhaps in her injured heart the tune is astray

In the floating speed of her ever-moving life-tide

It has effaced her burning sky, and given a profound peace

To the slumber of the desert sands.

Like the fragrance of my heart my love makes thee beauteous

And that drifts down day and night

Adown the long lotus-stem onto the petals . . . .

The mind's sky fills with a sigh in the long afternoon

Closing the door of the petal, the perfume of the lotus wafts alone

Where, no one knows.

Leaving behind the sweet smell of discarded petals

The mind floats, its sweet breath following free

I do not know where—

As I sit here in the dark shadow of night.

I cannot see the petals, today the tired arteries are in fiery celebration.

Only I alone feel

Thine lost scent, fragrant breath,

Only on my heart's cornice appears thine welkin, heavy with sleep.

The mind is entranced, wrapped in the fragrance.

I know not when it forgot

The sweet timid casement of the jasmine,

Or whom it seeks, far afar, breaking open the prison-doors.

On the bank of the evening breeze

Tearing asunder the darkness

Comes slumber.

It seems pure make-believe,

This seeking for you.

Even then the tide pulls

As the wide-awake realization strikes at the heart of sleep.

What intolerable pain fills me with fragrance!

I float far out on a tide of wild camellias

Leaving behind the suffering body, the mind roams abroad—

In the south breeze

It loses itself as it moves on in eager reassurance.

A fistful of dust remains, as does a very erroneous vanity.

The whole conscience, the spirit, the edge of the mind, are pained.

The comely, rounded form of the jasmine mingles in the dust

Making white petals bloom, diffusing abundant fragrance

In a tempest of wild henna, murmuring fragrantly

Forgetting the intense pull of the whirlpool, scent of the mind
She tears at the form of the petal to seek
the fragrance deep inside . . . .
Now
A garden of fiery blossoms wakes in the still wind
All talk and music have come to a stop
Thine lost memories have brought forth this storm that fills the sky.
'Tis mine love that makes thee beauteous
The fragrance of the mind—
That drops day and night upon the petals
Her fragrance, fraught with pain, wafts like peaceful sleep
Onto my mind's sky.

THE GALLINULE

(Original: Dahuk)

The gallinule called all night . . . .

This is the Land of Nod, the still pool of deep sleep!

I've stayed awake alone all this night long.

Let the dice game of deception be today,

And let the day-bee sleep on a weary branch.

Listen attentively today to the gallinule's call.

The moon leaves the starry port, floating on to the ocean of the night

Floating continuously under cover of feathery clouds

Like a tireless diver dipping into the ocean again and again

Lifting out the dreamy corals.

The drowsiness on the wings of the dew

Falls out unhindered,

And the blue sky-palace of the Fairy Queen

Becomes quieter and quieter

As the lamp of desire is extinguished.

Only the gallinule calls out restlessly.

A Call as profound as Death comes up from the depths of the ocean

Plumbed by a diver, as incorporeal as a ghost-bird

And the stars light up sleepily across a dreamy sky.

Art thou still awake?

Art thou indeed all ears to listen?

Art thou listening to the ebb of those skyward words?

He alone stands sentinel awake in that dense forest of sleep.

His dream-fairy follows her own wakeful route

In the slow wind, with a very sleepy companion indeed.

The melody of the gallinule's call spills out of the full goblet of Night.

Only the melody floats

As the moon wanes over the night-sky, full of melancholy dreams

In the cane thicket.

It seems thou art only an incorporeal melody.

Even then, I know thou art not the tune

Thou art only the instrument. Thou art an intoxicating draught.

Thou only carry the sweet notes of the deep sea, interred

In the thick, sky-gathering forest.

The sad blue moonlight dims when the gallinule calls.

O Bird! O Goblet! I've failed to know who thou art, yet.

Maybe I do know who thou art, with that patterned form

And those lovely colors, tarred with a strange brush.

However, I fail to recognize the wine

Making the edges of night weep

Of which the hurtful essence makes intense pain gather

On the rim of the forest

And the separation of night gathers on the nipa and common palm.

I cannot recall that tune.

I think thou carry the full goblet of that wine,

O Cupbearer!

Draining the dregs of that wine carafe, brimful of melodies

At the very rim of the copse

So very quietly alone.

O goblet of unfamiliar wine!

The thirst of that wine makes the unknown land of the sun

Eagerly agog,

Even though that sun itself is right now held captive

In the casement of the dark night.

The eastern horizon is bathed now in a song of radiance
And the youth of the seven heavens is unsullied.
Then sing out in full throated ease at the fount of the blue tides.
O Bird, let this lethargy of thine abate
And thine unclean thinness be effaced
Along with the dark night—at the eroding window.
Let the search for the horizon
And the fiery song begin again
The pink throat of thine she-parrot will not be covered
And her pink scarf will be spread out
In the starry copse of the blue sky, in a sweet dream
In the walnut wood, almond and apricot groves.

EVENING AT PORT
(Original: Bandarey Sandhya)

The stately stag was liquid brown, like the dusk.

The moon floated in on his curved antlers,

The only restless light among the seven seas;

The night-hunter shoots an arrow from his dark bow.

The tide of the Arabian Sea keeps on calling to lands far afar.

Dusk has lost the pink hue of daylight from her face

And here the stag brings the new moon

In on his antlers, heralding Ramadan.

The full moon in her abundant youth waits

For the thin crescent of the new moon.

In the sixteen-year-old's fullness of youth

Of sixteen blooming petals

Came a guest: a weary traveler of the port.

In the entranced dream of the fiery companion of the sunset

Is a lone call to her blossoming interior.

This dew has waxed dreamy on numerous seashores

Where stars like gold flowers tumble to the courtyard of night.

AT THE CASEMENT
(Original: Jharokay)

Into the unmoving casement of the downcast blue cup of sky
Blended the faint sound of the wayfaring crowd.
Upon the ashen mountain disappeared the flowery flame of fire.
Weary from its blind circling that fierce burn
Is the mere memory of the forest dells.
Leaving the branch of the sandpaper tree to
the far-off jasmine, of the henna,
Or perhaps one of the thousand and one nights of Baghdad
Descended.
O dearest Shaherzadi, what unknown love
Makes thee so embarrassed and furtive today?
All thine love wants to hide again
Behind the veil.
In vain thine diamond jewelery tinkles sweetly.
O Seductress, thou snatch away the weary fog of sleep
From men and their manhood.
Thou, coral-lipped one, scatter
Pollen, fragrant with the sweet scent of saffron.
This night is dark and deep! The mind
Seeks that fragrance out
Like a wayfaring upwind floating in on the south breeze.
Rending the sky asunder
At the north seashore in the south sea typhoon.

Like birds in the monsoon

She moves about hither and yon

Seeking her nest.

The fragrance wafts in from far afar.

O Dearest! Here I am, afloat on the deep blue tide

Of a very long new Spring.

I float, concentrating on the signs of the stars,

On the wings of a profound melody

On a still night.

Circling the fields of cane, tearing the sea of darkness to shreds

To the portal of the moon.

The wine whose intense burn floats thee on the choppy sea

On the storm of stars in the field,

That tune makes faded feathers fall off.

Flashes of lightning color thine lack-luster form.

Inklings of comets flash by beside thee like arrows.

The storm of the blue sea raises an unfettered, restless tumult

On the canopy of the dead forest.

Even then, so tranquilly do thou pluck up the tune of the night

From the deep impassable bottom of the deep sea.

The call of the gallinule . . .

It is as if all complaints and sorrows

Gradually fade into nothingness.

O untiring bird! In the forest of the night

Thou keep calling as thou goest

Like a chainless freedom.

We who are bowed down in heavy chains

Hear not thine melody; instead

We injure our bodies and minds

With our own poisoned bites.

Thou art not of these faint unclean souls,

Thou carry the complete melody of life and death

In thine fully liberated mind.

So art thou of free wings, and introverted,

O Gallinule,

That can call out, emptying so full a heart. We cannot.

On the strings of the bamboo vines the wind plays his lyre;

Eventually that stops, too

As the moon sets behind ancient forests

And the darkness thickens.

We sit face to face

In the deep shadowy moment of every grief.

The night drips on dewy leaves,

At the shores of life and death

In silent sorrow.

Piercing the heart of that all-pervading darkness

Some weary voice calls the call of the thirsty gallinule

Only in the far off forest.

THESE NIGHTS
(Original: Ei Shob Ratri)

These nights are for speaking intently to ourselves
The old wayfarers who are guests of the dust today stand behind us.
The joke of the skeleton that Kaikhushrau dreamt of is futile.
Long since are the days when his corpse nourished the germs.
Even Shahriyar watches as his desires fall unfulfilled by the roadside,
As the deep emptiness of a life bound in chains overtakes him.
These nights are for candid speech—
Where by the edge of fast flowing life the
dark sand dunes stand immobile
With the unmoving travelers at the bottom,
Their bodies sere, shadowy and cold
Smiting all songs, all dialogue as barren and frigid
Tolerating the power of the tomb, yea, and of the sand as well.
These nights listen intently to that conversation,
As in their dark rambunctious winds fly the stars.
The goblets of these darknesses, and the marble veils
With diamond flecks sprinkled, sparkle in Zulaikha's dream
And in Lailee's red wine. By the casement of Canaan
The pink moon falls by the sand dunes of darkness.
These nights just meditate intently
To hear again the calls of the Koh-i-Toor and Safa.
The far-travelling caravan, by the sound of the camel-bells
By starlight melts into the heights of the Marwa.
Speaking in the dim whiteness of a light dream
This scarcely perceptible whiteness of the fading night
Wants to be morning.

AT THE OLD SHRINE
(Original: Purana Majare)

At the old shrine, a few human bones lie
Listening to the call of a night-bird.
Their deep night thickens further as memories descend.
These nights are for earnest conversations with ourselves.
I know that the wayfarer is a guest of the dust
Who had seen through myriad illusions and pleasure.
The comely world
Has as collected memories the futile dirge of his life.
The call of the night-bird: the accumulated mound of darkness
Seems a sandbank, on either side of which waves
The fast tide of life. On the lifeless white sands
The drum plays on, right beside the shroud.
Beside the ancient bricks, some listen to numberless errors
That have fallen undefeated into the many abysses of death.
The call of the night-bird makes this old shrine quake.

THE PILOT

(Original: Panjeri)

O Captain, how far is it to the first light of day?
Behold, hidden behind massive clouds, your welkin.
Have the stars and the moon not risen yet?
With you on the mast, I absently row along.
A plumbless fog engulfs all this emptiness.
O Captain, how far is the dawn?
To the dark horizon of what river have we arrived
After the weary voyage of a long night?
What a dark blue shadow of life
Raises such a lament of a wounded heart in a tempest-weary vision
That the drumbeat of life gets fainter and fainter before fading away?
With you up on the mast, I row along absently
Observing just the endless fog before me.
O Captain, is it not morning yet?
The travelers count their days at port
Listening to the sound of our ship as if through the seasonal breezes
And seeing our sails through the enchanted veil of the moonlight.
Oh, these weary travelers
Stay awake on the seashore
Painting hopelessness onto their fortunes.
Where are we off to, to what fathomless distance,
Sailing these wayward ocean-currents?
Around the shore the travelers crowd,
With you on the mast, I absently row along

Through the dim darkness of a lonesome night.
O Captain, how far indeed is the sunlit morn?
Only through negligence and false desires
Have we picked up illusion enough to drown ourselves in.
For our mistakes, the travelers huddle near the water
Gazing fearfully out at the darkness
As their sun and moon have set already.
In our play, their insipid night of misfortune
Crumbled weeping to the dust.
We've raised laments in the group of merchants.
From house to homestead rises the sound of weeping
That we have heard.
Ah, is that the lament of the wind, or is that
The crying of the hungry?
Is that the roar of the sea, or the suffering of the oppressed?
O, in what famished ribs does the victory-tabor of death sound?
O Captain! Wake up and behold the fierce scowl of testimony at port.
Wake up to the scowls of countless hungry mouths
And look, look out to see how far it is to the rising sun.

THE GOLDEN EAGLE
(Original: Sworno Eagle)

The eagle which has crost the pinnacle of Al Burj,
With the speed of lightning and a tempest in her wings,
Has fallen to the dust on broken wings, being trodden on
By the vain demons, in dire neglect.
Those golden wings and that body are lying today in the dust.
The companion of light and air, fearless rider on the tempest,
Sees today the approach of her own death, she at death's door
And her massive gravestone beside the bottomless well.
The sun has set today beyond the shores of Oxus,
Bringing massed grief in the approaching dusk—
And the cruel mountain of mistakes closed the way off.
There is no wind beside this expansive field.
This night, like a python, has swallowed up all the light,
As if Rustam wakes alone with Sohrab's corpse.

THE CORPSE
(Original: Lash)

Where the wide road turns the corner,
Where the pitch-black surface has not turned dusty,
Just there, by the roadside, a corpse with its face hidden
Has fallen on the ground.
I know the evening crowd never keeps note
Of that dead person.
I know that corpses of men with hidden faces
Lie on the dust,
Immobile with hunger, the body with its pulses heating
Has fallen to the ground.
Well dressed men and women, like so many devils,
Walk right on by.
The stone chamber, prison of death,
The skilled courtesan with her face made up
Has opened the door in cordial welcome
While some are oppressing the world by ruling with an iron hand
As is being observed on the street,
Where five and a half feet of bones are
forming the graves of the dead.
The dead humanity lies in the dust with it, its face hidden.
The sky has been secreted in the pillars and columns of the vain.
Daily with their bloated bellies
They are dying here with their faces in the dust.
This supernatural beastly vanity, inhuman and crooked
Like brazen robbers

Is robbing the eternal human soul, the rights of man,
And closing the door, snatching away their morsel of food.
They construct their playhouse today with human bones;
The testimony lies right here, in this dust, with face hidden.
This bloated, barbaric civilization,
This bestiality,
This most crooked curse of the century,
Is poisoning this everyday world,
And the night sky.
What is this civilization that mocks the ultimate spirit
Of man today?
What devil ridicules man by throwing him
Into the coil of death today?
What Lucifer today kicks at the corpse of man?
Which specter laughs raucously,
Drenching his unsightly body in the wine of human blood?
The groans of man fill the air from sky to sky.
What propensity holds them in its thralls today?
What Devil is inflicting dirt and mud
On pristine rose-petals?
Who fills the colorful firmament of sky with venomous desires?
Who takes the hand of woman to use her as a sex object?
Of what civilization, indeed, are they?
Who cuts through the rib to play dance music?
Who makes workers bleed to fill up his goblet?
Of what civilization, indeed, are they?
When indeed has man sacrificed himself to thee,
That thou revenge thyself,
O Devil of the senile civilization?
Thou drink the blood of babes with a smile on thy face,
And molest the bodies of raped women unhesitatingly,

Ascending the steps of the crowd with no trouble at all
Thou leave them by the wayside drain.
O senile civilization turned pauper
Whose servant art thou?
Or are some beasts thine serving folk?
What a lowly rung of humanity,
Whose torture has made naught of peace,
The earthen hut and the living grave,
Lying with their face hidden upon the earth.
Those well dressed ones who serve this senile civilization,
Whose footfalls make this earth and the sky groan out loud,
Don't look to see what dirty, foul-smelling feces
Mix with their spirits to mingle with the beasts.
What adulteration makes the dog and the she-dog
Deceive each other with knives of distrust
And bring forth bastards to be trampled underfoot by civilization?
Signaling with their thighs, their women march towards death today
As do the torturing men,
With the enormous hunger of greed driving them
To drive them far below the path of humanity,
Towards a profound demise.
The terror of their oppression has devoured the abode of peace
Where the sere corpse lies, biting the dust
Of Senile Civilization.
The swollen-fatted oppressors are servants of a dead civilization.
Go today with the curses of man.
Then, when it's time, we shall kick thy
chained flesh all the world over
And pull thee to the door of the deepest hell.
Bear today the curse of the oppressed, death-scarred earth.
May thou be destroyed,
Be destroyed.

THE STORM
(Original: Tufan)

"Swift as an arrow flashed the unstoppable wave
Saying, 'Here I am, at the moment I speed.
When I lose my speed I am no more."
—Iqbal

That tempest has stilled, that fierce wing of the Simoom
In the cold, sun-storm effaced night of the Sahara,
Near the ferocious fangs of the blind mute
darkness coiled like a python.
The intense rays of the distant traveling Bedouin
is today hidden under cloud cover
And his flag of victory is buried in the desert sands.
That tempest that has lost its velocity and
mixed into the sand, formless
Counting its final days in the deadly famine.
Shrouded in hunger is its all-consuming cloak of death.
But no! I know that great fire of life has not been put out.
O Strong One! If thou come down this way just a bit,
If thou, Seeker, stand at the edge of this dead desert,
If thou canst infuse speed into this procession of men,
Then they will be able to pull up this storm effortlessly
And unleash the unfettered emotion of
the Sahara onto this dead field.

O STANDARD BEARER

(Original: Hey Nishanbahi)

Has the flag fallen to the ground in the storm today,
That eternal half-moon victory standard?
Has the victorious flag of the first day bowed
To the great apocalyptic pain of numerous deaths?
Who are those standard bearers, crawling along?
Whose cries fill the void of earth and water?
Has the flag fallen to the ground today,
Does the flag-bearer touch the ground as he goes along,
And is there a massive impediment at his head,
That crushes the heart under a mountain of thick lies?
O Standard Bearer, the night is ahead of thee today.
Does the deep dusk of that dark scarf block thy sight?
Even today the rocky road of sand dunes is there before thee
And the crowded beaches harbor no friend for thee.
Behold the ark of the sun in the tide of formless radiance
That tears through this night in a sharp storm of light!
The run-off of ice-melt at the touch of the light
Tears asunder this icy-frozen, endlessly frigid dark night.
Hast thou not awakened to new life when the light touched thee?
Has life not come forth from the corpse,
And has the sun not broken through thy body yet?
Has the sun indeed not broken through the confines of this night,
And is thy road shrouded as yet in dusky darkness?

O Standard Bearer! Is it for this
That thou art bent over today?
Is it thus that the standard skims the ground?
Even yet, I know, thy advance heralds the sunrise.
Thine sky, sun and light are shrouded
In a curtain of black fog.
Sparks of the searing hot desert sands fly up underfoot
And instantly disappear far off at each trot the horse takes.
Freedom flies blood-red at the flaming pinnacle of the wind
With the pacific symbol of the new moon on the white flag.
That unstoppable wave of conflict does not brook any hindrance,
And sparks fly from its hooves every instant.
In this flood of light, who is the herald bearing the flag
And breaking through centuries-old fog with the force of a storm?
Awaken me beside thine road,
Awaken me on this empty field,
Awaken me where the soldiers are.
The sun does not concede to restraints,
Awaken me where that Madinatun Nabi shines forth,
A world of pity, and a liberty as red as an injured lotus
Is borne by the white flag of that fragrant mind.
Today I see the insipid night build and destroy there
Death's lethargy takes over at the moment the petal opens.
Where is the flag? Where have those days
ridden on the wings of Time?
The desert dust bears the memory of that exploration.
The nights of this senile wolfish land are dreamless
And lances are held aloft here to guard against big obstacles.
O Standard Bearer! The sharp clip-clops of horses' hooves
Are not heard here,
And the whimpers of numberless famished mouths

Cannot be counted.

Where is the inauguration of thy hero-companion?

The blank mind returns today in the despairing wind.

Thy flag, fallen to the ground, does not wave in the storm

And thy companions fall dead of senility everywhere.

O Standard Bearer! Even then fly thine half-moon

And break over and over the death embankment of night's portal

Perhaps the clash of weapons will not sound here today

And the broken spine will be apprehensive, fearing death;

O Standard Bearer! Fly, fly even then,

Spread moonbeams from sky to sky.

If thine flag flies not

And maybe falls to the dust in a fierce storm

Even then the dreams of the day are on this dusty road.

I know that this procession will break apart

the confines of party,

Clasping the world in a victorious fist,

And, unlocking the dark of the night,

Will wake the sun in the blue sky.

Even now the inkling of far distance wakes in thy eyes

The great possibility of discovering a sea-route

And of coming down after traversing the sky in an instant

To listen to the Earth's music

Is still there in thee, O Inattentive One!

Thou art still alive, thou still live in the soldier's sword;

The half-moon bearing the crescent is still thy companion.

That unheard melody is in every atom of thy being

Where the awakened human spirit beholds a sea of tears.

It has a bank; be not afraid on the shore of that sea

O Bearer of the half-moon standard, prithee keep this plea of mine

Where the sea in fierce hunger is as blue as night

And where the eddying tide is itself a huge blockade.

THE FLAG
(Original: Nishan)

O mine flag, flag mine with the half-moon!

One day thou brought forth life, in force and flood.

Thou art the rider on Khalid's arms, of the Zulfiqar

O Unfading One, on Omar's path to the world

Thou hast traversed open grassland and high hills jutting straight up

When once thou rode on a strong wrist.

Weak arms are unable to bear that burthen

The flag of humanity does not wave upon a wounded heart,

Thus is it that everywhere around she beholds her own death today.

O New Moon, whose hand carries thee aloft today?

There lies the sere field of Arafat, without Bil'al.

So the minaret of day and the edge of the horizon are both downcast.

I cannot fly this mine flag there.

Or perhaps faith is today crippled into weakness

And the standard of the struggle has ceased flying

Here we are today, puppets in Lucifer's hands

We are faithless, so our dead souls carry

The burthen of our lust,

So the brink of day keeps sliding farther away

To the deaf-blind brink of death, where a chain appears

And the body and mind are sore with iron rule and terror,

So today I call upon thee, O Calm One!

O bright release from darkness, ever unmoving!

Return thou to these hands.

O traveler to Hera

With the living soul of the Safa and the Marwa

O Commander, burn through this dead habitation

And break down this impassable portal to death.

O Flag, please give us again the inkling of humanity.

O Flag, indicate the path that the dead travelers must follow,

And point out the sign of the full moon

Which signals the milk of human kindness.

Where the gasp has risen

From the heart of a people devoid of humanity

THE FLAGMAN

(Original: Nishan Bardar)

The burthen of days and nights has today become unbearably heavy.
The strayed wayfarer is readying himself for a journey back.
The forest all around echoes with the right to life amongst the dead.
O Flagman, unfurl thine flag here.
The night of sorrow thickens; the dark is opaque.
Now is the time to bring out thine flag of light right here.
With a solar storm tearing through the dead leaves of this darkness,
On the shores of death fly the bright flame of thine first dawn
And float the fog of sere moss in this tempest of light.
Somewhere in an empty field flies thine banner.
Among the throngs is an empty branch here;
The bird of its dreams has taken wing long since.
Senile and unmoving, it keeps moaning, O Flagman!
He whose journey had begun with Abraham,
Who found sanctuary with the Holy Prophet (PBUH),
Bears the flag of the Elixir of Life
Traversing the field to bring the fragrance of camphor.
Thou bring that inkling of light, breaking down this dark portal,
And return it to this soul of the dead forest.
Laat and Manaat have broken up in the liberated Ka'aba today,
Even then they twain have changed
To take up residence in countless hearts.
In the marrow of the poles is the night of Senility of A'd and Samud.

Where is the envoy of light?

A'd and Samud wake with reared heads in the thicket of thorns.

Some breathe poison all around,

Some bear the wine of death in their skulls,

Corpses upon corpses come in a crowd

With destruction in their skeleton mouths.

That bestiality has spread its hood today,

Poisoning even a distant possibility.

One thrash from its tail breaks down the plant of dreams.

The devil dances with Laat and Manaat—

Only half alive;

In his faded sky the rainbow has gone black out.

The lost nightingale of the Portal Tree

To the Seventh Heaven

Now dirties the dust of this earth every moment.

Digging her hole in dusky darkness,

She has turned this bright day into a vapid night.

The infertile house of nightmares on dry soil

Trembles anon at her raucous screams.

Her daytime sky is fearful, and her slumber full of terror

As the desert simoom smites her trampled nest.

The building rises with her heart's blood.

With her skeleton the tormentor measures the road to the minaret.

Listen to her laments echoing everywhere, O Flagman.

Fly, fly thine flag here, O Hero!

There is only the dusk of night here, and the darkness thickens.

Bring out thine sunshine here.

On the branches of the populace rises a yearning for life.

Bring on vivacity to quench this deep thirst they have

As the ocean tides, O Flagman!

THE CHILD
(Original: Aulad)

The sailor has come through the swish of many storms.
Many are the famished nights at sea that have agitated him.
He's lost his way in the dark.
Heralds of death have circled around, calling to him.
The sweaty hopelessness of despair, filling his broken hull,
Has risen in him, while ahead called the ferocious dark sea.
Even so, the sailor found a haven in an unfamiliar world.
Even as his eyne are filled with the black terror of nightmares
And his colorless lips have the taste of death upon them,
Even if the broken hull of his dilapidated bark is full of victory today,
Behind him woke only the hunter of that unbearable dream.
He has brought in a full hold, braving numerous tempests.
The victorious Sinbad, Child of Man, has returned.
He is observing people's homes, living tombs
On the shores of an impassable sea in an unknown land,
Where in the farce of congealed stone
The dead desert soul of haughty man has taken up residence.
Row on row, line by line
March those carrying burdens
With pick-axes and shovels,
Pens and ploughs.
On weary feet march the wayfarers
Including children famished in hunger, their spines withered,
And numerous caravans
Traversing deserts, fields and forests

Like a farce in man's courthouse.
Crowds of children march on, lifting to their lips
The acridly tasteless goblet of life,
The hungry children of man at death's door.
The stony road to immobility,
The trenched road of this horrible civilization
Covers the sky in darkness and calls out to them.
What trench is this?
Here burns only the flame of a hungry day
Spewing out poisonous smoke, that carries
The grotesque horror of death,
The burden of a suffering mind, measureless deep pain
In the midst of which moves the dead child of man, kicked around,
In fear of Lucifer, in the grotesque tomb, in a complicated hole.
The crowd of children marches on towards an epidemic
In the crooked, ugly edge of the dark road to ruin
Where at every bend the Devil has set traps.
Towards that, in an irresistible attraction
The sere, weak children of man march today.
I see the corpses of hungry children on the road
And right next to them, the wine of the wealthy
Spilling right over.
I see ferocious famine knocking on the farmer's door
I see the scarlet letter flashing on the foreheads of the downtrodden
The ridicule of the vain have made slaves of men
And of women, fallen prostitutes.
The base of man is far afar,
And here the tide reaches out.
The crooked serpent of immobility has called out
To those who are here,
Having lost their way in the whirlpool,

And it is thus that these have been blinded
To the centuries-old civilization and have gone astray.
By increasing the quick ones, they will
supplement the misguided ones
In the hands of killer men
And with killer women too.
Their blood has quickened, turning them
Into tormentors and hunters,
These inhuman dead children of man.
With chained feet their breath of life stops—
The farce that freezes stone in the court of man.
This time
Not in this human court symbolizing the neuter,
Nor yet on the muddy black road the Devils tread,
This time our complaint
Is for the court of God the Almighty
The complaint of this fallen hungry mankind.
I know many civilizations have crumbled to dust, many Samuds,
And yea, many Pharaohs and devilishly cruel Nimrods
Have mingled into dust.
A new group of travelers appeared on the impassable rocks,
Flying the flag,
And bringing with them the untiring storm of life.
Their tabors are sounding today
As their victorious turbans wave in the air.
We hear only their voices.
May the beat of their hearts in their courageous breasts
Never be racked with pain
Or made to quake with fear.
I see the traps of torture on the road.
May the children of man
Never be led down the wrong path again.

THE SAILOR OF THE SEVEN SEAS

(Original: Sat Sagorer Majhi)

I know not how many dark curtains were
opened to let the morning light in.
In the orange grove the green leaves quiver.
The flood tides of the seven seas have brought
the foam to thine doorstep,
And even yet thou awaken not? What, not yet?
O Sailor of the Seven Seas, hark the ship that calls at thy door!
An immovable picture is she, standing absolutely still.
There is no way for her to go, her sails don't fly.
O Sailor! Please honor mine entreaty!
Rise up, rise up among the boatswains
And thou wilt see thine boat afloat on the sea again.
Like a full moon over the blue sea
Cutting through waves of cloud and breaking down barriers.
Even yet, awaken, for the blooming lotus has
faded long since in the morning.
Art thou asleep yet? Not awake, even now?
Dost thou hear the snake hissing at the door?
The famished have gathered there in numbers
O Sailor, list! Give away thine merchandise
Or everything will break into bits and pieces.
Thou seest not, what will o' the wisp these folks follow
Ever downward, out of the way.

O boatman! Thou knowest thine star has not gone out.

This desert dreams of thy moonlit night.

See the Sweet Basil and the pink blossom gathered on thine horizon

Then why so fearful, trembling with an unknown terror?

Is thine ark destroyed?

Do the clouds hide thine stars,

And is the broken helm of the ship unable to steer?

Is this why thine empty sails, filled by the wind,

Tremble on the starving main?

I have no idea; even then I call upon thee,

O Sailor of the Seven Seas!

The coconut fronds of Coral Island swish in the wind.

Thine deckhands have no patience now to tolerate this slumber

And the Seven Seas spew forth foamy venom in black rage.

In the meantime, strangers travel the skyway

And in the orange grove the green leaves quiver.

Who fills thine coffers with marble in Marjan?

In sleep, thou hast only heard the pastorals of nightmares.

Have all the debts of the disobedient night not been paid off yet?

'Tis the morn. And thou art not awake yet?

Art thou sleeping, still?

Hast thou forgot the season of the clove-flower and the cardamom

Where the saffron light of day opens up in dust and stone,

And where Titania, Companion of Fairy Dreams,

Wakes, with a kiss for the charmed white jasmine?

Hast thou forgot that first voyage, when the ship set sail

For the land of strange flowers

And the dream of raising amethysts in all those eyne

Shining in the moonlight,

Where the ship, with sails unfurled

Cut through the salt water easily, forever seeking

Tearing through the blue veil of the horizon

And slicing the salt water

Sailing off who knows where?

I have no recollection which unknown port that ship docked at.

Even then I remember this much, that there in Marjan

The ship was filled with marble.

I know not when thy sails split in a messy storm,

Today the pythons of nightmares haunt thy dreams.

In thine flimsy ports of death they rear their hoods.

They have poisoned thine bowed welkin.

Even then, O Sailor of the Seven Seas, wilt thou hear yet once more

Thine closed door knock in the dry wind?

This is no murmur of dreams on the coconut fronds of moonlight,

Nor is this the window of fairyland, in the port of oranges.

Now thine closed door resounds with human laments

With the cries of hungry babes twanging like notes from the sitar.

These torn sails have to be filled and raised today

These torn sails will now have to be patched.

Let everyone clap upon seeing the broken masthead

Even so, the ship will have to sail today.

Who knows when thine dream-entranced night waned?

The winds of a fierce storm whip at the door today

In his snaky tongue is an inkling of death

With one ferocious strike of his tail he breaks down
thine colorful minaret.

O Sailor, stop thou not even then, beholding this sign of death

Even then thou hast to float this ship on this centuries-dead sea.

Night has now descended here

Even so, the royal gates of Hera are visible yet, far afar . . .

A pebbled path,

Such impediments of mountains and oceans,

The crawl of the specter of midday.

The vulture flies overhead, casting shadows.

We have lost all the grassy fields and flowering gardens,

Even so, the royal gates of Hera are visible yet, far afar . . .

All the segments of the royal gate have opened long since

The moonlight of the twelfth night has swayed there long since.

O helmsman! Wilt thou not weigh anchor?

Is it not time yet?

O Sailor! Wilt thou not unfurl thy sails?

How much later will that be?

Thine sails are blowing in the wind,

So don't be late this time.

If the salt water has touched thine hull

Tarry thou not

This time play the trumpet of thine voyage

And let the wayfaring passengers come, O Boatman, be not tardy.

Thou knowest, it is very late already

And many boat-floating monsoons have passed.

How the numerous cardamom seeds have scattered in the storm!

The wind has stolen the fragrance of myrrh.

Death has thee now by the throat.

The sea-foam laps thine doorstep,

And all of thine hasnuhana has long since tumbled to the ground.

All the fragrance has dropped off in the garden,

Even if the orange grove is still green with leaves

And its days slowly approach the end.

By the endless profound attraction of unknown lands

Green dreams bring forth the grayness—
He knows this, this is familiar to him.
Even so, he shall awaken the pink grapefruit in all its blush
Even as the brown leaves tumble to the ground in the air,
Even as cold death drips all around him.
Even now endless hope glows in him, and he has big dreams.
O Boatman! Be thou not fearful yet
And glean thou the amazement of the wayfaring stars of Hera.
Let tumble the orange leaves in this storm—yet still
Myriad leaves crowd where the royal gates of Hera have opened.
Even as the desert has to be crost by this road
And the salt sea water has risen to that path.
There is shelter there, I know, with shady trees
And sweet fresh water.
Unfurl the sails then, weigh anchor;
O Seeker, I know that now after so many roads
The portal of Hera shall rise before thee.
Then do weigh anchor and unfurl the sails.
Trim thou the sails.